Aloha 'Oe

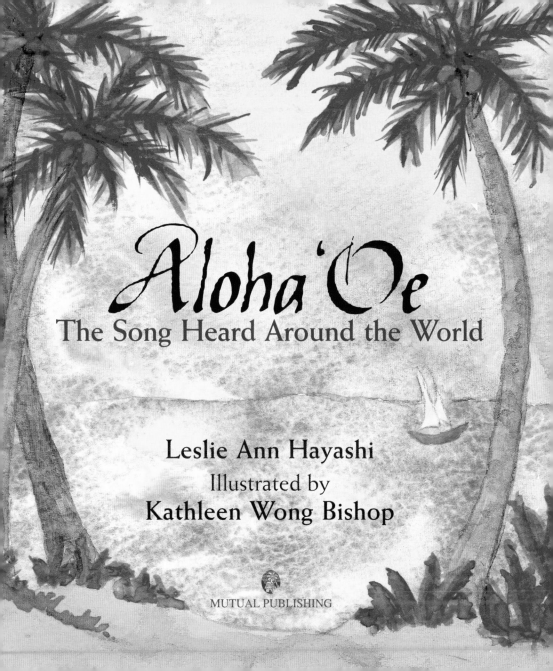

Aloha 'Oe
The Song Heard Around the World

Leslie Ann Hayashi

Illustrated by
Kathleen Wong Bishop

MUTUAL PUBLISHING

ISBN 1-56647-696-8
Library of Congress Catalog Card Number: 2004110944

Design by Mardee Domingo Melton

First Printing, October 2004

Mutual Publishing, LLC
1215 Center Street, Suite 210
Honolulu, Hawai'i 96816
Ph: 808-732-1709
Fax: 808-734-4094
email: mutual@mutualpublishing.com
www.mutualpublishing.com

Printed in Korea

---| DEDICATION |---

Lydia Lili'u Loloku Walani Kamaka'eha Pākī Dominis
September 2, 1838 to November 11, 1917

*Mahalo nui loa for your enduring gift of music
and for your genuine love of Hawai'i's people.*

"Aloha 'oe, aloha 'oe
Farewell to thee,
farewell to thee...."

Who has not heard the sweet refrain of this song and felt their hearts touched by this enchanting melody?

Laden with lei, loved ones are bid a fond farewell.

The year is 1878 and the composer is Lydia Lili'u Dominis, wife of O'ahu's governor, John Owen Dominis. Born forty years earlier to Anale'a Keohokālole and high Chief Caesar Kapa'akea, Lydia's parents followed the royal or *ali'i* tradition of entrusting their daughter to be raised by adoptive parents. Laura Konia and Abner Pākī became Lydia's *hānai* parents.

However, the song may never have been created if Lydia hadn't received musical training at a tender age.

Princess Lydia Lili'u Dominis composed *Aloha 'Oe* during her most prolific song writing period.

While enrolled in the Chiefs' Children School,
Lydia learned the Western system of musical notation.

By the time she was four, Lydia's formal music education had already begun. Like other children of the *ali'i* class, Lydia boarded at the Chiefs' Children School, later known as the Royal School. Taught by American missionaries, this school was established to educate the next generation of the nation's leaders.

Over the years, Lydia developed perfect pitch and her ability to sight read was well known. Handed music to new songs, Lydia sang them, allowing other students to memorize them. She also learned to play numerous instruments including the guitar, piano, organ, autoharp, and zither—her favorite instrument. Of composing, she said it was as natural as breathing.

As a member of Hawai'i's royalty, it was expected that Lydia would compose. Her older brother, King Kalākaua, also wrote many songs, including *Hawai'i Pono'i*, which would later become Hawai'i's national and state anthem. Their younger sister, Miriam Likelike, and younger brother, William Pitt Leleiōhoku, also produced several popular songs.

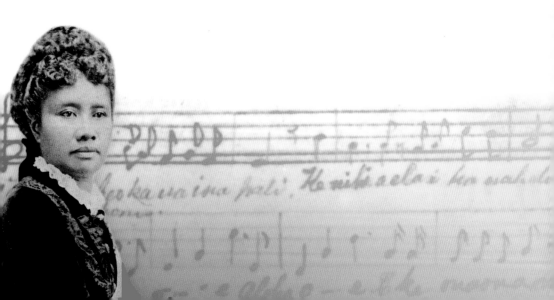

Lydia's older brother King David Kalākaua was a Renaissance
man displaying a wide range of talents including writing songs.

"Discovered" in 1778 by Captain James Cook, by the end of the nineteenth century, Honolulu Harbor had become a busy international port due to its central location in the Pacific Ocean.

15

A second element necessary for *Aloha 'Oe* to come into existence was someone to arrange and promote the song. The bandmaster who would accomplish these two tasks arrived in Hawai'i in 1872 as a result of a naval frigate damaged three years earlier.

In 1869 the *S.M. Donau*, the first Austro-Hungarian ship to visit Hawai'i, entered Honolulu Harbor with engine damage. While the ship underwent repairs, its crew performed many concerts to the delight of the public. Citizens then petitioned King Kamehameha V to revitalize Hawai'i's own band which had been created in 1836.

*P*ersuaded by influential Germans living in Hawai'i, the King contacted Germany to find a bandmaster. Ultimately Captain Heinrich Berger, the assistant bandmaster in the Second Life Guards, one of two elite infantry regiments of Prussia, was dispatched to the Hawaiian Islands in June 1872. Berger would serve under four monarchs and become the longest serving bandmaster.

Bernard Lanan painted this portrait of 28-year-old Captain Heinrich Berger, shortly after Berger first arrived in the Islands.

Captain Berger turned out to be a fortunate choice as the leader for the royal band. Having played under Johann Strauss, the "waltz king," Henry Berger introduced many waltzes, polkas, marches, and ballads to the islands. Over the next forty-three years, Captain Berger would compose more than seventy songs, arrange over two hundred songs (including *Aloha 'Oe*), and conduct an astounding thirty-two thousand concerts. It is no wonder Lydia dubbed him the "Father of Hawaiian Music."

Captain Henry Berger and the Royal Hawaiian Military
Band on the steps of the 'Iolani Palace in 1887.

Immigrants walked across the China Bridge to Quarantine Island, later named Sand Island, where they stayed after arriving from their homelands in Asia.

*A*s bandmaster, Berger played at every notable and historical event in the islands. In addition to conducting the King's Concerts on a regular basis, he also performed in honor of visiting royalty, for the islands' socialites, and for newly-arrived contract labor immigrants. Quarantined for eighteen days and far from their homelands, the workers were grateful for his music which helped to pass the time before they were sent to various plantations around the islands.

Two particular songs may have played an important part in the creation of *Aloha 'Oe's* tune. Some claim the song's melody resembles a tune written by Charles Crozat Converse and published in the 1850s, entitled *Rock Beside the Sea* or *Lone Rock by the Sea*. Others note the chorus is similar to George Frederick Root's composition, *There's Music in the Air,* also published in the 1850s. Still others contend the song was actually written by Captain Berger, a claim he vehemently denied. However, he later composed *Aloha 'Oe March* which used part of *Aloha 'Oe's* tune.

With a composer and a bandmaster in place, the last element necessary to create the song was the special moment. The year is 1878. Lydia, her friends, and attendants are leaving Colonel Edwin Boyd's sprawling Maunawili Ranch nestled against the Koʻolau Mountains on the windward side of Oʻahu. They mount their horses and ride along the ranch's carriage road lined with majestic royal palm trees. Ahead lies the steep Pali trail back to their homes in Honolulu. Red and yellow ʻapapane birds flutter among the blossoms, trees, and bushes. The sun slips lower in the sky, bathing the valley in a golden mist.

*C*olonel Edwin Boyd stops to receive a lei from a young lady. Lydia catches sight of the couple saying goodbye in the twilight and watches their fond embrace as they part. The image of the tender farewell stays with her and a song forms in her heart. Soon she is humming the melody.

*N*ear the top of the winding trail, Lydia turns to take one last look at the beauty below. The lush emerald greenery is embraced by the sapphire and turquoise waters of Kāneʻohe Bay. Homeward bound, a young ʻiʻiwi bird pulls the early evening behind it.

As they descend into Nuʻuanu valley, rain sweeps against the steep, verdant Pali cliffs. Closer to the trail, the mist glides through the ʻāhihi lehua bushes laden with red blossoms. A cloud follows the entourage down into the valley like a wistful memory, a reminder of the beauty and love Lydia has witnessed. Others join in the Queen's humming. By the time the composer arrives home, her song is complete.

Aloha Oe.

Ha'aheo ka ua i na pali Ke nihi a'ela i ka nahele E uhai ana i ka liko Pua ahihi lehua
o uha Aloha o - e Aloha o - e ke onaona noho i ka lipo A fond embrace a hoi ae au Until we meet again

2-

O ke hali'a koha i hiki mai
Ke hone ae nei ku'u manawa
Oe no ka'u ipo aloha
A loko ea ku a'e nei

Chorus

3

Maopopo ku'u ike i ka nani
Na pua rose o Maunawili
I laila hia'ai na manu
Miki'ala i ka nani o ka liko

Composed at Maunawili 1878. Played by the Royal Hawaiian Band in San Francisco August 1883 and became very popular.

1st Proudly swept the rain by the cliffs
As on it glided through the trees
Still fol'wing ever the liko
The Ahihi Lehua of the Vale.

   Chorus. Farewell to thee, farewell to thee
      Thou charming one who dwell in shaded bowers
     One fond embrace ere I depart.
     Until we meet again

2d Thus sweet memories come back to me
Bringing fresh remembrance of the past
Dearest one, yes, thou art mine own,
From thee, true love shall never depart.

3d I have seen and watched thy loveliness
Thou sweet Rose of Maunawili
And 'tis there the birds oft love to dwell
And sip the honey from thy lips.

Lydia's handwritten version of *Aloha 'Oe*.

Hawaiian Bar

Captain Henry Berger conducted public concerts regularly at Queen Emma Square, Thomas Square, and, later, at the 'Iolani Palace Bandstand after it was built.

*F*ive years later, in August 1883, *Aloha 'Oe* made its mainland debut in San Francisco under the direction of Captain Berger. The Hawaiian Kingdom's Royal Hawaiian Military Band had been invited to compete in the Knights Templars Conclave contest. Sung by Madame Nani Alapai, the band's first female vocalist, the song captivated the judges and won first prize. And so *Aloha 'Oe* began its journey around the world.

Within a year, *Aloha 'Oe* was published in Hawaiian, German, and English and could be heard in German harbors and in chalets nestled in the tall peaks of the Swiss Alps. The composer, her song, and the islands were closely linked.

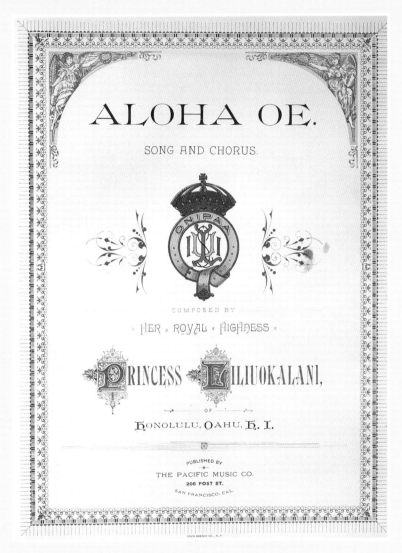

In 1889 the Princess asked family friend Charles B. Wilson
to help her copyright several of her songs including *Aloha 'Oe*.

King Kalākaua invited Princess Lydia to accompany
his wife, Queen Kapiʻolani (seated), and to represent the
kingdom at Queen Victoria's Golden Jubilee
celebrating her fifty year reign.

*I*n 1887, Princess Lydia accompanied Queen Kapiʻolani to England to attend Queen Victoria's Golden Jubilee. En route, Hawaiʻi's royalty visited various cities across the United States. In Washington, D.C., the royal party dined with President Grover Cleveland.

During their stay in Boston, the city hosted a grand reception in their honor featuring the Boston Cadet Band playing *Aloha ʻOe March*, an interpretation of *Aloha ʻOe*.

While in London, the Princess met many rulers and dignitaries from various countries including Denmark, Prussia, Persia, Siam, India, Belgium, and Japan. All had traveled to England to celebrate Queen Victoria's fifty years as the reigning monarch of England, Ireland, and India. In the Hawaiian tradition, the Princess created special songs to commemorate the event.

*B*ack in Hawai'i, Captain Berger began the tradition of performing for the steamers arriving and departing from Honolulu Harbor. By the time he retired in 1915, Bandmaster Berger conducted 2,062 pier-side concerts, serenading visitors from all over the world with the song's unforgettable melody. And on June 30, 1915, Berger lifted his baton for the very last time to direct the tender strains of *Aloha 'Oe* as his own farewell song.

The arrival and departure of visitors from
Honolulu Harbor were major events.

*W*hat started as an enchanting love song also became known as a bittersweet farewell song for the monarchy. In 1891 Lydia Kamaka'eha succeeded her brother King Kalākaua after he passed away while visiting San Francisco. When she assumed the throne, the composer took the name given to her by the King in 1877 when he designated her heir apparent: Lili'uokalani.

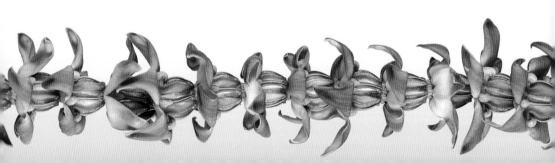

Princess Lydia ascended to the throne as Hawai'i's only
female monarch in 1891 following King Kalākaua's passing.

To avoid bloodshed, Queen Lili'uokalani stepped down from the throne, allowing the Provisional Government headed by Sanford Dole to govern the Islands.

In less than two years, Queen Liliʻuokalani reluctantly yielded her power to the "superior force" of the Provisional Government. Despite appeals and one attempt to restore the monarchy, the Queen abdicated the throne in 1895, forever ending Hawaiʻi's monarchy.

However, the Queen continued to seek support to reinstate the sovereign nation, including traveling to Washington, D.C., to meet with President Grover Cleveland. During her seven-month stay, she also compiled a book of her songs entitled *He Buke Mele Hawaiʻi*. One copy was sent to Queen Victoria and the other she delivered to the Library of Congress.

Following an unsuccessful attempt to restore
the monarchy by a group of her loyal sup-
porters, the Queen was subsequently arrested and
tried for treason in 1895 by a military tribunal.
Convicted of a lesser charge of concealment of treason,
her five-year jail sentence was later reduced by
Governor Sanford Ballard Dole to eight months
confinement inside 'Iolani Palace; five months confinement at Washington Place, her residence; and
another eight months confinement to the island of
O'ahu. Many mistakenly believe Queen Lili'uokalani
composed *Aloha 'Oe* during those sad times.

Queen Lili'uokalani is escorted up the stairs of 'Iolani Palace to face
treason charges before a military tribunal. Opposite page: 'Iolani Palace.

The Royal Hawaiian Band brought the music
of the islands to eager audiences everywhere.

With the establishment of the new govern-ment, the band was no longer a military band and shortened its name to the Royal Hawaiian Band, a name retained to this day. Under the direction of Captain Berger, the band resumed its travels to the neighbor islands as well as to the mainland, including a trip to the Chicago Fair in 1895. Ten years later, in 1905, the Band performed at the Lewis and Clark Exposition in Portland, Oregon. *Aloha 'Oe* was always included in the Band's repertoire of songs.

*C*onsidered to be the first Hawaiian hit song outside of Hawai'i, *Aloha 'Oe* sheet music was widely published across the United States mainland. By the late 1920s, *Aloha 'Oe* sheet music reached the shores of Japan.

Since it was composed, *Aloha 'Oe* has been immortalized in other songs, literature, plays, movies, and even cartoons. With each new medium, *Aloha 'Oe* remained an enduring favorite.

This sheet music of *Aloha 'Oe* published in 1908 depicts a fond farewell.

*T*n December 1908, Jack London, a frequent visitor to Hawai'i during his short life, wrote a bittersweet love story entitled *Aloha 'Oe*. In the story, Dorothy Sambrooke, accompanying her father on a month-long trip to the islands, falls in love with Steve Knight, a young man who is one-fourth Hawaiian. Everywhere the young lovers go, *Aloha 'Oe* serenades them.

Weeks later, as Dorothy stands next to the railing on the departing steamer, thousands of voices sing, *"My love to you. My love be with you till we meet again."* When her father, a prominent United States senator, explains that Steve won't be able to visit her because he is of mixed ancestry, she is devastated. Spotting Steve in the surging crowd below, Dorothy flings her lei to him and then turns her head to cry on her father's shoulder, her sobs drowned by the song's refrain.

Jack London, a famous American author,
found inspiration in the Islands.

*A*loha 'Oe's popularity destined it for Broadway and ultimately Hollywood's silver screen. On January 8, 1912, *The Bird of Paradise* opened on Broadway in New York. Written by Richard Walton Tully, the play was about an American sailor who fell in love with a young Polynesian woman. In addition to *Aloha 'Oe*, other Hawaiian songs were featured. The opening cast included five Hawaiian musicians playing ancient Hawaiian musical instruments such as the ipu (gourd), accompanied by the 'ukulele and steel guitar. Audiences across the country and in Canada were introduced to Hawaiian music for several years while the play toured.

In 1919, a *Bird of Paradise Show* featuring Joseph Kekuku, the Hawaiian musician who invented the steel guitar and developed its unique technique, traveled the European continent. As a result, *Aloha 'Oe* played on a steel guitar became synonymous with Hawaiian music.

In addition to *Aloha 'Oe*, *The Bird of Paradise* play featured other popular Hawaiian songs including *Waialae* and *Mauna Kea*.

A vintage post card shows the famous Moana Hotel on the shores of Waikīkī Beach and the lovely melody of *Aloha 'Oe*.

*L*ater two movie versions of Tully's play were made. Busby Berkeley, a famous choreographer and director, directed the dances for the 1932 version of *The Bird of Paradise*, creating an extravagant, exotic, and lavish tropical spectacle. Starring Delores Del Rio and Joel McCrea and filmed in Hawai'i, the movie was considered one of the most expensive films made during this time.

By the early twentieth century, Hawai'i had become an extremely popular vacation destination for visitors from all over the world. Songwriters everywhere used *Aloha 'Oe* or parts of it in their own compositions. Jack Frost penned a song entitled *Aloha 'Oe, Aloha 'Oe* in 1915. Berton Braley's humorous poem, *Don't Play Aloha 'Oe When I Go*, written in 1923, was later set to music.

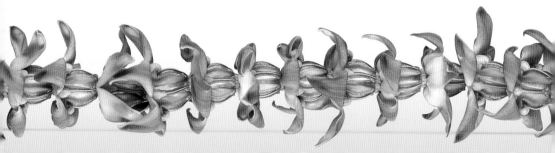

*T*homas Alva Edison, America's greatest inventor, visited the islands. His phonograph had become commercially successful and with the advent of this new medium, *Aloha 'Oe* once again was heard around the world. Edison's close friend, Henry Ford, the automobile manufacturer, hired five Hawaiian musicians, Henry Kailimai, Frank Kema, William Lincoln, Robert Waialeale, and Gordon Piianaia, known as the Ford Hawaiian Quintet, to perform authentic Hawaiian music in Detroit, Michigan. Later this group traveled to New York to record several albums for Edison's recording studio.

Early record companies such as Columbia, Edison, Imperial, Pathe, and Victor produced massive numbers of recordings featuring Hawaiian music during this time. *Aloha 'Oe* found its way onto various recordings, among them Pathe's recording of Irene Greenus singing *Aloha 'Oe* in 1917.

Sheet music from 1912.

This photo of Queen Liliu'okalani, at age seventy-five, was taken in 1913. The Queen remained gracious and compassionate throughout her life.

On November 11, 1917, Queen Liliʻuokalani, the song's composer, passed away at the age of seventy-nine . Her stately funeral befitted the last ruler of the Hawaiian Kingdom. However, *Aloha ʻOe* was not among the Queen's compositions played at her services. Earlier, when the Queen learned that *Aloha ʻOe* had been played at someone's funeral, she became upset, stating emphatically that she never intended her composition as anything but a love song.

Almost ten years later, on October 14, 1929, when news of Henry Berger's passing spread, bands and symphony orchestras in the United States and Europe played *Aloha ʻOe* as their opening number in tribute to the song's arranger and promoter, yet the song itself was also omitted from Berger's funeral services.

Following World War I, hapa-haole music, literally translated as "half-foreign," an exotic blend of English and Hawaiian and sometimes gibberish lyrics, became extremely popular. The *Honolulu Hicki-Boola-Boo; Hapa Haole Hula Girl; O, How She Could Yacki Hacki Wicki Wacki Woo,* and *The Cockeyed Mayor of Kaunakakai* were classic examples. Al Jolson, an early talking movies star, introduced movie goers to *Yaaka Hula Hickey Dula (Hawaiian Love Song)*, in which he used parts of *Aloha 'Oe.*

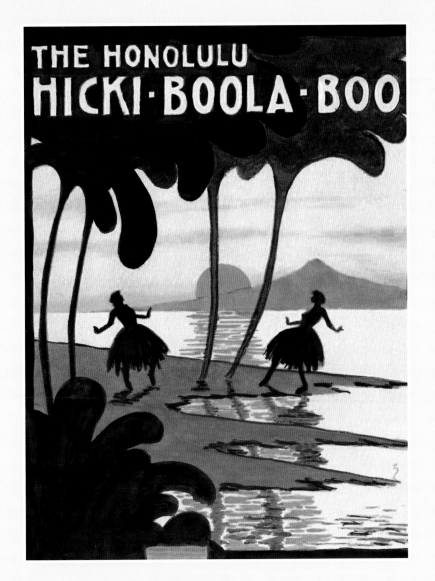

Sheet music from 1916.

Hollywood produced the film, *Waikiki Wedding*, starring Bing Crosby.
The setting in this photo is Nānākuli on the leeward coast of Oʻahu.

With the success of the early talking movies, newsreels and cartoons were added. Paramount, Merrie Melodies, Looney Tunes, and Amos 'n Andy cartoons were among those using well-known songs such as Stephen Foster's *Camptown Races* and Johann Strauss' *Blue Danube* in their sound tracks. Soon *Aloha 'Oe* became part of this repertoire of popular songs which arrangers used to accompany tropical scenes and departures.

From the 1930s through the 1950s, cartoon characters such as Daffy Duck, Bugs Bunny, and others wearing grass skirts were heard singing *Aloha 'Oe*, exposing new generations of adults and children to the song's melody. *Aloha 'Oe* became synonymous not only with Hawai'i, but all of the South Seas and ultimately the idea of paradise itself.

At the 1932 Olympic Games in Los Angeles, *Aloha 'Oe* was sung in the closing moments of the ceremony as the flame in the Olympic torch was extinguished. Three years later, a radio program hosted by Webley Edwards began regular broadcasts of live performances from the Banyan Court of the Moana Hotel, the "First Lady of Waikīkī," a stately Victorian inspired hotel located on Waikīkī Beach. *Aloha 'Oe* was soon heard regularly in thousands of homes across the United States, on the Armed Forces radio programs as well as in South America, Africa, Mexico and as far south as New Zealand and Australia.

Farewell to Thee

Proudly swept the rain by the cliffs,
As on it glided through the trees,
Still fol'wing ever the liko,
The 'Āhihi lehua of the vale.

Chorus:
Farewell to thee, farewell to thee,
Thou charming one who dwell in shaded bow'rs.
One fond embrace, e'er I depart
Until we meet again.

'O ka hali'a aloha i hiki mai
Ke hone a'e nei ku'u manawa.
'O'oe nā ka'u ipo aloha,
A loko e hana nei

Maopopo ku'u 'ike i ka nani
Nā pua rose o Maunawili
I laila hia'ai nā manu
Miki'ala i ka nani o ka liko.

Thus sweet memories come back to me
Bringing fresh remembrances of the past.
Dearest one, yes, thou art mine own,
From thee, true love shall ne'er depart.

I have seen and watched thy loveliness
Thou sweet Rose of Maunawili
And 'tis there the birds oft-love to dwell
And sip the honey from thy lips.

These are the words as written in Queen Lili'uokalani's own hand, although a number
of variations of the song exist. The original version of the chorus' opening line is
sung quite differently than the familiar tune. The three syllables of "Aloha" are sung
in all the same note while "oe" is sung as "o-o-we" (phonetically oh-oh-way) with
each note higher than the last.

AUTHOR AND ILLUSTRATOR

Leslie Ann Hayashi is an award-winning judge and writer. **Kathleen Wong Bishop** is an artist and Christian educator. Friends since first grade, Leslie and Kathleen have written and illustrated a number of award-winning books together: *Fables from the Garden, Fables from the Sea,* and *Fables from the Deep.* They are currently working on *Fables Beneath the Rainbow* and other Hawai'i books. Their website address is: fablesfromthefriends.com.

Kathleen Wong Bishop (left) and Leslie Ann Hayashi on Aloha 'Oe Drive in Maunawili, O'ahu, not far from the Boyd Ranch where Princess Lydia was inspired to write *Aloha 'Oe*.

PHOTO CREDITS

Hawai'i State Archives
Pages 5, 7, 8, 11, 12, 17, 18, 28,
29, 33, 34, 40, 43, 44, 49, 56, 60, and 63

Kathleen Bishop
Pages 15, 21, 22, 25, 27, 69, and 71

Steiner Postcard Collection
Pages 30, 37, 39, and 52

www.hulapages.com
Pages 47, 51, 55, and 59

Alan Van Etten
Page 77

Luis Reyes
Page 67

*A special mahalo to Agnes G. Conrad,
the State of Hawai'i's first archivist,
for her invaluable assistance.*

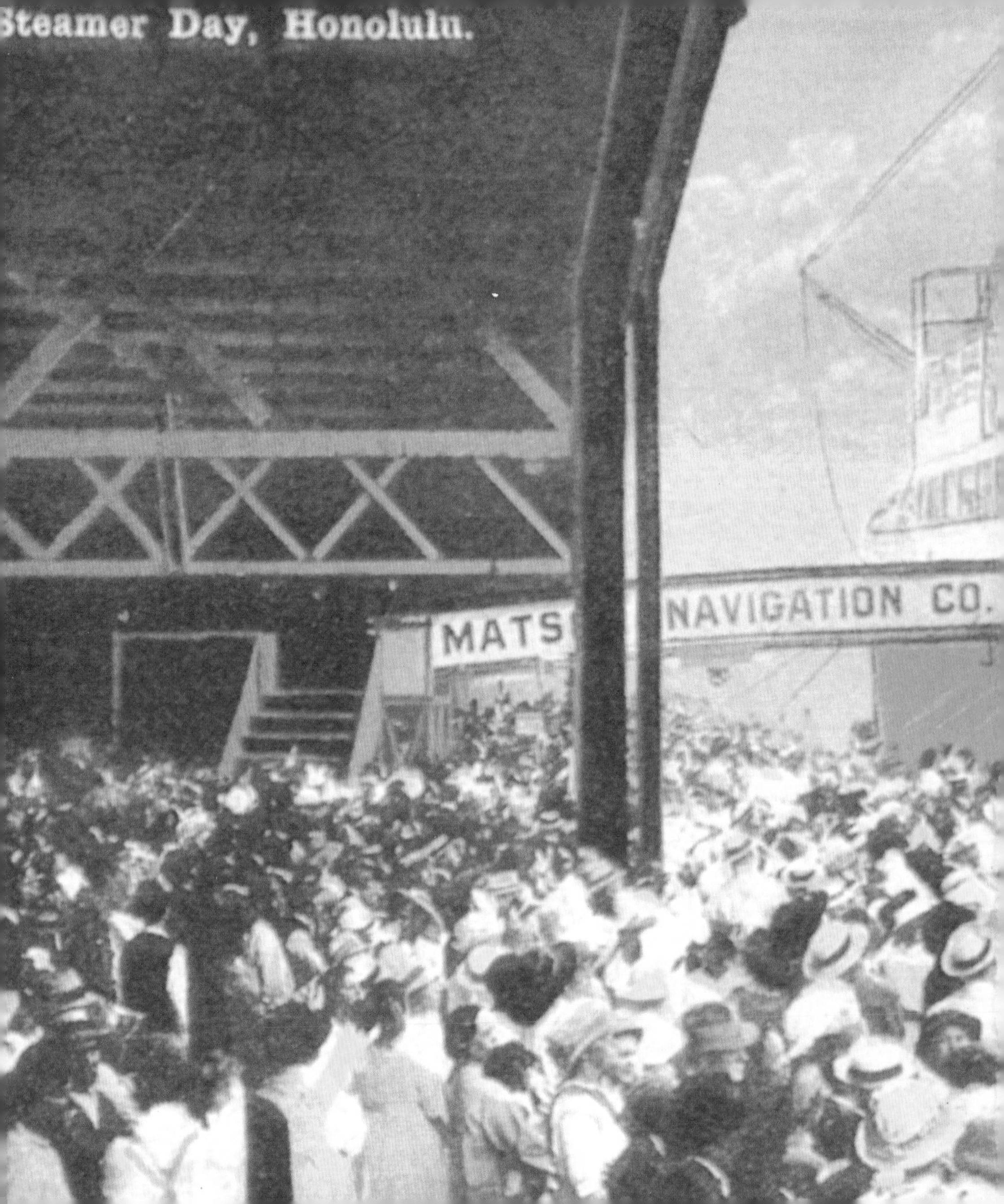
Steamer Day, Honolulu.
MATS
NAVIGATION CO.